Stop Burning Your Money!

Prologue

This is not a long book. That is by design. I had a college professor who once told me "you have an amazing capacity to pack very little meaning into a lot of words." That was good instruction. I hope this book is evidence that I learned the lesson. After reading this book, you might discover that the smallest book you ever read made the biggest difference in your future.

It contains valuable information you can use to get ahead financially and improve the quality of your life. These facts are most useful stated clearly and succinctly without unnecessary embellishment. For that reason the facts you want will be presented in the first chapter. You will discover exactly what to do and how to do it by the end of chapter 1.

The remaining chapters contain information and reflections intended to inspire you to actually use what you learned in the first chapter. The world is full of people who do not use what they learn. Something stops them from applying new knowledge to make a difference in their life. In fact, learning what to do and how to do it means nothing unless you actually change your habits and do it. It is not new knowledge that will improve your life. It is new actions that become new habits.

John Dryden said, "We first make our habits, and then our habits make us." I invite you to read the other chapters just as carefully as the first one. I hope you will find yourself inspired enough that nothing can stop you from using the facts you have learned to develop new habits that will produce the desired results for you.

PART ONE

How to DIRECT INVEST

$150 a month and earn $500,000

instead of smoking cigarettes.

Chapter 1 – Direct Investing: What to Do and How to Do It

What there is to do is simple. Buy stock in General Electric using the GE Direct stock purchase program, and have your dividends reinvested. You will find complete instructions on how to do this at the GE website. The web address for the web page you need is:

http://www.ge.com/investors/personal_investing/how_to_invest/index.html .

Just go to this web address and follow the instructions to setup your account and get started. Besides instructions to get started, you will find other useful information here. For example,

Average Annual Total Return

For the Five years ending 12/31/2007, GE Common Stock's Average Annual Total Return is 11.8%.

Dividends

In September 2008 the board approved management's plan to maintain GE's quarterly dividend of $0.31 per share through the end of 2009. GE last raised its dividend on December 11, 2007, from $0.28 quarterly to $0.31 quarterly. That dividend increase marked the 32nd consecutive year in which GE raised its dividend. GE has paid a dividend every quarter since 1899. GE's dividend yield is currently about 7%.

Preferred Stock

GE does not have any preferred stock outstanding that is available to the public.

However, GE does have $3 billion of perpetual preferred stock in a private offering to Berkshire Hathaway, Inc

The $3 billion preferred stock to Berkshire Hathaway is the General Electric stock Warren Buffet purchased in 2008.

For most people enrolling and buying online is the most convenient. However if you prefer to do this by phone, just call 800 STOCK GE (800 786 2543) toll free to enroll and get started.

Regardless of which method you select to enroll, be sure to select the option to have all your dividends reinvested. Also, you will need to download and read the prospectus first. Just click the prospectus link that looks like this

<u>Download the GE Stock Direct Prospectus</u>

near the top of the webpage to open, download and print the prospectus. If you are doing this by phone, ask the person on the phone to mail the prospectus and other paperwork including your enrollment application to you.

You may be wondering why I recommend GE stock instead of some other company you are interested in owning. The short answer is, I agree with Warren Buffet. He is arguably the most successful investor in history and he recently invested 3 billion dollars in GE stock. If you do your research on this company you will understand why. Careful analysis will reveal a PE ratio and a dividend yield that is amazing for an established blue chip company. Fundamental analysis indicates a well diversified company with a great balance of businesses including leading edge technologies like wind energy equipment. Technical analysis indicates positive trends for GE such as increasing money flow into GE stock. It is apparent this company is solid and positioned to survive the current global economic challenges all large companies are facing. GE can be expected to thrive long term as it has for more than a century. There simply is no valid reason to think otherwise.

If you would prefer to own stock in a different company, there are many other companies that offer a direct investment option similar to General Electric which allows investors to have their dividends reinvested. Feel free to modify this plan by substituting a different company if you like. To begin your research of other companies that offer direct stock purchase plans, go to this website for a list of hundreds of companies you can check out.

http://www.wall-street.com/directlist.html

This site will give you access to information you can use to learn more about the direct investment approach and many companies worthy of your consideration as a potential investor. Make sure the company you select has a good track record of paying dividends. Also, compare the fees they charge you to set up an account and buy stock directly. Finally, before deciding to select a different company, write a list of clearly stated reasons you want to invest in the other company instead of GE. If the reasons are valid, you will have no problem stating them clearly in writing.

On the other hand, if you find it difficult to write your reasons clearly and succinctly, that may be an indication your reasons are either invalid or unclear. If so, you should probably stay with GE.

Chapter 2 – Why Direct Invest

Does it make more sense to spend all that you earn every month, or make a small change in your lifestyle to save $150 a month and over time earn a small fortune?

If you smoke, do this instead of smoking. You will live longer and be healthier so you can enjoy the small fortune you earn even more. After all, what good is a small fortune if you forfeit your health?

If you are not a smoker, find something else you can give up to save $150 a month. Perhaps soft drinks and snacks, or a cell phone, refinance your car to lower the payment, or trade for a less expensive car. Spend less on restaurants, movies and other forms of entertainment that are not essential. If you commit to do the program, you will find the place to save the money. If you cannot see any way to save the money, consider a part time job to earn a little extra money. If you are serious about earning a small fortune, get serious about deciding how to do this and do not give up until you find the solution that works for you.

Once you have decided how to generate the money to invest, the primary reason to utilize the direct invest approach is to increase your profit on the investment. Why pay high fees and commissions to a stock broker to own the same stock you can buy directly and own it for less of your money? Obviously if you spend less to own the asset your return on investment is higher.

Unfortunately, most stock brokers and financial planners do not tell their clients about this option because they do not earn fees and commissions if their client decides to direct invest. So be smarter than stock brokers and financial planners and choose the investment that works better for you, not for them.

To get a sense of the value of direct investing versus paying broker fee's and commissions, consider the charts below carefully.

Results Summary	
Starting amount	$250
Years	30
Additional contributions	$150 per month
Rate of return	11.80% compounded monthly
Total amount you will have contributed	$54,250
Total interest	$460,649
Total at end of investment	**$514,899**

Savings Balance by Year

Year	Additions	Interest	Balance
Start	$250		$250
1	$1,800	$150	$2,200
2	$1,800	$393	$4,394
3	$1,800	$667	$6,861
4	$1,800	$974	$9,635
5	$1,800	$1,320	$12,755
6	$1,800	$1,708	$16,263
7	$1,800	$2,146	$20,209
8	$1,800	$2,637	$24,646
9	$1,800	$3,190	$29,636
10	$1,800	$3,812	$35,248
11	$1,800	$4,511	$41,559
12	$1,800	$5,297	$48,656
13	$1,800	$6,182	$56,638
14	$1,800	$7,176	$65,614
15	$1,800	$8,295	$75,708
16	$1,800	$9,552	$87,061
17	$1,800	$10,967	$99,827
18	$1,800	$12,557	$114,185
19	$1,800	$14,346	$130,331
20	$1,800	$16,358	$148,489
21	$1,800	$18,620	$168,909
22	$1,800	$21,165	$191,874
23	$1,800	$24,026	$217,700
24	$1,800	$27,244	$246,744
25	$1,800	$30,862	$279,406
26	$1,800	$34,932	$316,138
27	$1,800	$39,509	$357,447
28	$1,800	$44,656	$403,902
29	$1,800	$50,444	$456,146
30	$1,800	$56,953	$514,899

This illustration is very informative. Although your actual returns will vary since annualized returns fluctuate, this shows clearly the potential of the direct investing approach. Depending upon your actual returns, it may take more or less time to accomplish your goal of accumulating $500,000.

Here are some powerful questions for you to reflect upon as you decide what to do with the information in this book.

First, why should I do this?

The best answer to the first question is actually the second question.

Why not? What else are you going to do differently going forward that will give you a better opportunity to get where you want to go in life? If you have a better plan, do that. If not do this. Just don't keep settling for doing nothing or doing less than this.

Third, why not you? Some people are already taking advantage of this information and using it to improve their life. More people will start doing it going forward. Do you want to become one of the people who knew about this possibility but never did it? I hope not. Why not become the person you will have to be to get this done? You will not only make a small fortune. You will become a more powerful, successful and effective person. What else will you be doing for the rest of your life that is more valuable than that?

Fourth, why not now? There is no time like the present to make a decision that will alter your future dramatically. If you do not do it now, it is unlikely you will do it later. I invite you to make this moment a turning point to a better future for yourself and the people you care about.

Finally, what if this does not work? Ah yes, but on the other hand, what if it does?

PART
TWO

The Technology of Accomplishment

Unleashing Your Capacity

To Produce the Results You Desire

Chapter 4 – Accomplishment or Disappointment

Are you ready to stop burning your money? Are you interested in earning $500,000? In the past have you ever been interested in taking on a big project to improve your life and failed to get it done? Most of us have had this experience. Some people feel that every time they try to do something to make a big difference in the quality of their life they end up disappointed, having failed to accomplish their goals. Have you ever felt this way?

Unfortunately this type of feeling causes too many of us to resign ourselves to settle for whatever we have already accomplished in life and stop trying to find ways to improve our lives, our situations and ourselves. As a result of this resignation, we can avoid the pain of additional disappointment. However we also can miss real opportunities to *go for it* and build a better future for ourselves and the people we love.

If you find yourself stuck in your present situation, unable or unwilling to go for it again, something is stopping you from hoping for something more in life and making it happen. I do not want this problem to prevent you from using what you discovered in this book to make a profound difference in your life.

The technology of accomplishment is an approach you can use to get past whatever is stopping you from setting and accomplishing big goals. It is a way to free yourself from resignation and go for it again. You can actually use what you learn in this book to take powerful action and form new habits that can take you to a place you really want to go, but you were not on track to get there.

Has anyone ever told you to plan your work and work your plan? Have you heard other advice about setting your goals and formulating action plans to accomplish them? That approach to accomplishment works for a small segment of the people in the world, but how is it working for you?

Some people find this type of goal setting and problem solving very useful. But many of us do not. In fact, we often get stuck trying to figure out how to do it so we can write an effective game plan to accomplish our goals. The problem for us is that we get stuck trying to figure out how to do it, and we never get it done. For us there is another approach to producing results that is more useful.

The premise behind this alternate approach is that the key to accomplishing your goals is not figuring out how to get it done. Rather you must generate a powerful enough set of *reasons why* you want to do it. The implication is that when you fail to accomplish your goals, it is because you did not have clear and compelling reasons why to do it that were powerful enough to inspire you to persist until you succeed. Conversely, when your reasons why to do something are powerful enough, you will never get stuck trying to figure out how to do it and give up.

In the final analysis it is a matter of getting first things first. First focus on generating powerful reasons why to do what you want to do. When your reasons why are clear and powerful enough, your innate creativity and resourcefulness will be unleashed. You will begin to see clearly what there is to do next, and you will find yourself inspired to do it, rather than stuck trying to figure out what needs to happen after that.

The steps you will need to follow to start using this approach to accomplishing your goals are contained in the checklist on the next page. Read it carefully. Then read it again. Bookmark the page and keep the book in a special place so you can review it easily every day and reflect for a few moments. This process will empower you. The daily reflection on the content of your work as you complete these steps is an essential component in technology of accomplishment.

The Technology of Accomplishment Checklist

To Begin

1. Notice the desires that inspire you and make a list.
2. Choose the desires from your list you find most empowering.
3. Delete the items you can be complete without from your list.
4. Write your promise to pursue the remaining items passionately as if your quality of life is at stake.
5. Make another list of all the reasons why you want the things on your list of desires that inspire you.

To Do Daily

1. Begin each day reflecting on what you want and why.
2. Focus your attention on your reasons why.
3. Release your attachment to the outcome.
4. Shift your attitude to allow the universe to handle the details, declaring everything beyond your control is a detail.
5. Notice what there is to do next and do it.

Here are some examples of items you might find on one's list of desires that inspire her:

- Find a secure job with a promising future.
- Increase my savings by $150 per month starting now.
- Achieve financial freedom.
- Own a home that is paid for.
- Live abroad for 2 years.
- Have a companion for life and a relationship that works.
- Become a non smoker.

Here are some examples of *reasons why:*

- To become the person I will have to be to get them done.
- To know I am living in pursuit of my dreams.
- To become one who finishes big goals.
- To make the contribution only I can to others.
- To awake eager to live each day, not dreading it.
- To be proud of my work and myself.
- To transform my relationships with the people I love.

Here is an example of a promise to pursue goals passionately:

I promise to devote myself to the relentless pursuit of these goals recognizing that doing so is the only way to have the quality of life I want. I declare this is my destiny. Until now I have been stuck in the morass too often. While in the morass I forfeit my quality of life as well as my capacity to produce the desired results. Going forward I will use the technology of accomplishment daily to pursue the possibilities I treasure. I will invest my time, talent and effort going for it! As a result, *I will be complete while I accomplish my goals. My way of being will transform my quality of life as I continue my journey and fulfill the destiny I chose.*

Use the next few pages in this book to write your list of desires, reasons why and your promise to pursue your desires passionately.

My List of Desires that Inspire Me

My List of Desires that Inspire Me

My List of Desires that Inspire Me

My Reasons Why to Do the Things on My List

My Reasons Why to Do the Things on My List

My Reasons Why to Do the Things on My List

My Promise to Pursue My Desires Passionately

My Promise to Pursue My Desires Passionately

Finally, I did not write an ending for this book. You will be writing it as you use the technology of accomplishment to get where you really want to go in life. To encourage you to go for it until you get where you want to go, I would suggest you take Lee Ann Womack's advice from one of her popular songs. Her lyric says,

> *"...when you have the choice to sit it out or dance,*
> *I hope you dance."*

If you have questions or comments about the information in this book, please email me at the address below. I would enjoy hearing about your journey.

My best regards,
William Wilder
williamwilder@me.com

www.ingramcontent.com/pod-product-compliance
Lightning Source LLC
Chambersburg PA
CBHW081247170526
45165CB00009B/3224